Cooking
with the
Fishers

*Amish Family Recipes
from the Pennsylvania Farmland*

John and Sylvia Fisher

Big Bear Publishing US
Ronks, Pennsylvania

First printing 2009

ISBN 978-0-9801215-1-3
LCCN 2008937325

ATTENTION CORPORATIONS, UNIVERSITIES, COLLEGES, AND PROFESSIONAL ORGANIZATIONS: Quantity discounts are available on bulk purchases of this book for educational, gift purposes, or as premiums for increasing magazine subscriptions or renewals. Special books or book excerpts can also be created to fit specific needs. For information, please contact Big Bear Publishing US, P.O. Box 191, Ronks, PA 17572; 717-768-4644.

TABLE OF CONTENTS

The Fisher Family

When you travel to the Pennsylvania farmland you might think you've stepped back in time. Since the early 18th century, when they first settled in the New World, generations of Amish families have farmed the local land, easily resisting modern innovations like electricity, the automobile, and indoor plumbing. Their daily life is a form of worship that separates them from worldly distractions. Faith and commitment to family and community are at the heart of their beliefs.

Now meet a typical Amish family—the Fishers!

John Fisher

John was born into the simple life in Ronks, PA, and grew up on the sixty-acre "Piggy Farm," situated about one mile from Intercourse. The farm's colorful name dates back to the boyhood of John's grandfather, Amos (1920–1985). Amos and his friends loved to imitate farm animals on their way to school. His pig noises must have been outstanding, because the nickname "Piggy" stuck to Amos and has passed down through two generations to "Piggy John." John doesn't mind at all. The pigs added to the fun of growing up in an idyllic natural landscape where mules and cows grazed in the pasture and watered at the creek, and a quiet pond offered many hours of play—after school and chores, of course.

Amos was an historian who loved spending time with the children and teaching them the old traditions. John vividly recalls visiting Roadside America with Grandfather Amos and the rest of the grandchildren. The elaborate rural village in miniature, with moving trains, speeding fire trucks, and bubbling fountains, delighted him just as his grandfather knew it would. On the way home they stopped at an old churchyard where Amos pointed out the names of many revered ancestors on the headstones. Grandfather Amos gave freely of his time and talents all of his life, to the benefit of his family and his community. Even after he retired, he fed the horses, drove the hay baler, and was generally an enormous help to John's dad.

In 1986, at the age of sixteen, John joined the Amish youth group, The Souvenirs. Two and a half years later his sister Barbie's best friend also joined. Her name was Sylvia, and John was smitten. It was a great setting for the couple to get to know each other. Soon they started dating and married on November 19, 1991. Today they are blessed with six beautiful, healthy children: Sarah Ann (16), Emma Mae (13), Amos (11), David Paul (9), Mervin (4), and Aaron James (2). A seventh child, Jonathan, would have been six this year. Sadly, he passed away shortly after he was born, but he is cherished in their hearts.

Though a carpenter before he married and a sometime roofer in later years, John would much rather work in the fields with his family. The Fishers raise sweet corn, tomatoes, spring onions, and red beets on their four-acre farm. The whole family chips in, tending the produce stand set up in front of their home. In order to offer a complete array of fruits and vegetables, they fill in the rows with additional seasonal crops bought at local auction.

The family also sells soft pretzels, fresh lemonade, and ice cream at the Plain & Fancy Farm, a local attraction with a country store and horse-and-buggy rides, plus an informative multimedia production about the Amish way of life. John's brother and parents live at the "home farm," where he grew up. The specialty at their stand is homemade root beer.

Sylvia Fisher

Sylvia grew up in Gordonville, PA. At about eight years old she started helping her dad in the barn, milking twenty-four cows and carrying the milk by hand in buckets. There were also calves and heifers to feed.

During the summertime, the entire family devoted their days to the produce patch, hoeing weeds, and picking and washing vegetables to sell at their home produce stand and at the Kitchen Kettle Village in

nearby Intercourse. It was a lot of hard work, but Sylvia, her brothers and sisters, and her parents, all enjoyed pitching in together and strengthening their family bond. The just-picked fruits of the garden were a special pleasure for young Sylvia. She appreciated the variety of color, texture, and shape, and the fresh and pungent aromas that rose to meet her—and she still does.

One day, Sylvia's eighth grade teacher gave the class an assignment: Write an essay on the topic, "What I would do if I had a million dollars." What was Sylvia's dream? She wanted to open up an ice cream and soft pretzel stand. Little did she know her dream would eventually come true. In the summer of 2006, she and John set up an ice cream and soft pretzel stand in the little red barn in front of their home. To her surprise, the business immediately took off and has continued to grow. Many hands make light work, and so John, both Fisher daughters, Sylvia's mother, and some neighbor girls also help tend the stand. With the farm, the children, the house, and sewing for the whole family, it's sometimes difficult to find time for the business too, but Sylvia and her family make it work.

Sylvia's girlhood dreams didn't include anything about produce, but after marriage and a house full of children, she's quite content to farm like her parents did. Selling produce and refreshments brings in some income, plus other benefits. Sylvia finds it a great way to meet new people, and that is a real pleasure for her. "We have learned that there are a lot of friendly people out there," she says. "Let us live in peace and always be kind and loving to each other."

Sarah Ann Fisher

Sarah Ann was born on August 15, 1992, and named after her mother's older (by eleven months) sister, Sarah Ann. As the oldest of the Fisher children, Sarah Ann is a huge help at home with laundry, yard work, and canning, but her talents shine in her art and cooking.

Winter is a great time for Sarah Ann to stock up on her original greeting cards, practice using the sewing machine, bake pretzels for her family, and create exciting new recipes. Tuesday through Saturday in the spring, she moves her specialty to the family's Plain & Fancy Farm shop, where she demonstrates the art of soft pretzel making for

the public. Customers are drawn by the divine smell of warm pretzels and can't wait to dunk them in Sarah Ann's specially prepared dips. Although it's hard to decide between the pretzels, the homemade chips, the hand-dipped ice cream, the fresh-squeezed lemonade, and the homemade root beer the Fisher family sells, Sarah Ann's beautifully designed greeting cards are an obvious choice.

In 2002, the family acquired a Halflinger horse named Beauty, which Sarah Ann helped train so she could be hitched up to the 4 x 8 foot cart. At first her dad drove with her, until Sarah Ann was in eighth grade and Beauty was no longer wild. Then Sarah Ann could drive by herself, hauling produce in from the field. Beauty's first colt didn't survive, but now there is a brand-new colt named Bethany, born February 4, 2008. She's a lovely little animal and Sarah Ann and her dad have started another round of training together.

Like her mom, Sarah Ann loves when people visit at the family's pretzel shop and roadside stand. As Sarah Ann says, "Everybody's welcome!"

Emma Mae Fisher

The smells and tastes of the kitchen are a special joy to Emma Mae, born January 23, 1995. Ever since she was little, she has loved to watch Sylvia cooking up magic and baking up a storm. Little Emma Mae would pull a chair up to the counter so she could observe her mom's every move. By the time Emma Mae had reached fifth grade in the Amish school, she had baked her very first cake, and by the sixth grade she was mixing pretzel dough at the family's pretzel shop. Now this was fun! She still helps out at the shop whenever she is needed.

Emma Mae's most recent passion is mastering homemade bread. Her family finds that the more she makes it, the better it gets. That sounds good to Emma Mae, whose motto is "Practice makes perfect." Her kitchen skills are really gaining momentum. In fact, she celebrated her thirteenth birthday by cooking a special meal for her family—potatoes, noodles, meatloaf, corn, carrots, Jell-O salad, and a delicious cake decorated with candles. You'll find the meatloaf and Jell-O salad recipes in this book.

Besides the family produce business, summer is a time for mowing the lawn, weeding the produce patch, babysitting, and cleaning. Emma Mae helps with all of it. Then after a full day's work, Dad makes a bonfire in the backyard and everybody gathers around to grill Emma Mae's favorite chicken and baked potatoes, and finish off with roasted marshmallows and s'mores. Pitch a tent and sleep under the stars, and you've got perfection.

Amos Fisher

Amos was the first boy born to Sylvia and John, on April 6, 1997. Though he weighed in at a solid eight pounds, he got off to a rough start. A blockage in his heart called for surgery and a twelve-day stay at the Hershey hospital. Now, at eleven years old, he is doing just great.

Amos loves the animals on his home farm. When it comes to milking the family's fifty cows he's a big help, but he has the most fun feeding the animals. His dad throws silage (feed treated in a silo) down into the cart and when it's full, Amos pushes the silage into a pail underneath the cart and brings it to the cows. There are times when a cow will buck him. Dinnertime can be hazardous.

David Paul Fisher

David Paul was born on January 12, 1999, and on his last birthday he hit a milestone. As soon as he turned nine he was allowed to sit with the big boys in church. Up until then he had to sit by his dad.

For a long time David Paul heard his parents talk about getting some goats. This sounded pretty good to him but it wasn't happening. Then one day his dad hitched up their horse Buster to the red produce wagon and off they went to fetch some goats from their friends, Aaron and Ruth Fisher (no relation). They picked out two fine billy goats, one black and white and the other brown and white, plus six nannies, and scooted them into dog kennels for the trip back home. David Paul just loved to play with the family's adorable new critters. They were so cute, nobody could resist them. In time they added five baby kids to their goat family, and David Paul participates in their care every day. Then there are the chickens, the dogs, the horses, the colts…there's always a lot to do on a farm!

Mervin Fisher

Mervin was born on June 13, 2004. He was welcomed with special joy, since Jonathan had passed away just two years earlier and David Paul was already five and a half years old. The family had missed having a baby in the house.

Four-year-old Mervin's main job is following his older brothers around. He also enjoys gathering eggs every evening and playing ball with his little brother, Aaron James. Mervin loves music. Often he can be heard singing "Over Jordan, Home in Glory."

Aaron James Fisher

Aaron James was born on September 26, 2006. Six days later a school shooting in the local village of Nickel Mines drew international attention. The event brought tragedy to the Amish community and resulted in an unprecedented outpouring of condolences from around the world. Having little Aaron James to care for was a special blessing at this difficult time.

Now two years old, Aaron James is still the baby of the house. He loves when his brothers and sisters play with him, but his favorite is a piggyback ride from Dad.

Aaron James stays busy walking and talking as much as anyone will allow. When Sarah Ann comes home from the pretzel shop, he runs up and asks her for a "pretz"—meaning pretzel, and she happily obliges. Aaron James is a quick study. Like Mervin, he follows his brothers around and loves to sing. But the similarity ends there. Aaron James' favorite song is "Only a Little Boy David."

Jonathan E. Fisher

The Fisher family would not be complete without mentioning Baby Jonathan, who was born on Friday, June 21, 2002, at the Lancaster General Women & Babies Hospital. He weighed just 5 lb. 3 oz. and died of complications the very same day. He is gone, but never forgotten.

In Memory of Our Dear Little Rosebud

God had a rose garden that was very fair. He watched over it and tenderly cared for it.

One day He had a need for a beautiful rosebud. He walked through the garden looking for him....."Oh, this will be very hard on the stem, but he is the very one I need." When God reached out to take the lovely rosebud, some admirers of the stem said, "This is a perfect rose, we want to see him bloom. The rosebud is so fair, we need him here." God said, "You see, just today, I see all of time and eternity."

When he was broken off the stem, the remaining roses on it shook and shuddered and bowed down. The break went deep. God took special care of the wounded stem and watched over it. He and His workers gave it extra attention. After many days when God came walking through the garden, He came to the stem where the rose was taken and He said, "Ah, just as I planned, the ones that remain are fairer still."

Here, for the first time, and in the Amish tradition of lending a helping hand, the Fisher family has opened up their recipe file to the public. Now you can cook up delicious farmland dishes at home in your own kitchen.

All of the Fishers—John and Sylvia, and their children Sarah Ann, Emma Mae, Amos, David Paul, Mervin, and Aaron James—feel very blessed and they wish the same for you! Enjoy!

CHAPTER 1

Beverages

Fresh-Squeezed Lemonade

5 lemons
2 cups sugar
1 gallon refrigerated cold water
1 large pitcher

Cut the lemons in half and squeeze into the pitcher. Add the sugar and let stand for a half hour. Pour on the cold water and stir to mix. Chill and serve.

Iced Coffee

¼ cup boiling water
2 tbsp. instant coffee
½ cup sugar
12 ice cubes
2 quarts cold milk
ice cream (optional)
2½–3 quart container with tight lid

Dissolve the coffee and sugar in the water. Stir in the ice until melted. Add the milk. Pour into the container, tighten the lid, and shake well. Serve in mugs. Top with ice cream of your choice, if desired.

Orange Cream Drink

1 cup orange juice
1½ cups water
⅔ cup sugar
2 cups milk (or Homemade Vanilla Ice Cream, page 72)
12 ice cubes

Combine all the ingredients, pour into glasses, and serve.

Slush Punch

2 cups boiling water
1 cup sugar
1-16 oz. pkg. strawberry Jell-O
1-6 oz. can frozen orange juice
1 large can pineapple juice
1 cup cold water
2 quarts (or more) ginger ale
2-gallon container with lid

Pour the sugar and Jell-O into the boiling water and mix until dissolved. Stir in the frozen orange juice until melted. Add the pineapple juice and blend well. Then add the cold water and secure the lid. Freeze. About 2 hours before serving, add 2 or more quarts of ginger ale. Makes a little more than 4 quarts total.

Sparkling Punch

1-6 oz. can frozen lemonade

1-6 oz. bottle Hawaiian Punch

2-6 oz. cans frozen orange juice

2 quarts cold water

2 quarts ginger ale (or Seven-Up)

Stir all the ingredients together. Chill. Makes almost 4½ quarts.

Tea to Freeze

4 quarts water

4 cups sugar

4 cups fresh tea leaves

Boil the water and remove it from the heat. Steep the tea leaves for 15 minutes to make a concentrated tea. Discard the leaves. Add the sugar and cool. To serve, mix one part of the concentrate with three parts cold water. The concentrate may be frozen in 1-pint containers.

CHAPTER 2

Snacks & Treats

Hot Wings

4 lb. whole chicken wings
3 cups flour
a gallon ziplock plastic bag
vegetable oil to cover
¼ cup butter
¼ cup honey
¼ cup barbeque sauce
4–6 tbsp. hot pepper sauce
3 tbsp. apple cider vinegar
3 tbsp. yellow mustard
¼ tsp. garlic salt
blue cheese dressing (or ranch dressing)

Cut each wing into three sections. Discard the wing tip. Place the flour in the plastic bag. Dip the wings into the flour and deep fry on both sides until golden brown. Drain on paper towels. Place in a large bowl.

In a saucepan, combine the next seven ingredients and cook over medium heat until almost boiling. Pour over the cooked wings and let stand 5 minutes. Remove the wings from the sauce and place in a large baking pan. Bake at 350° for 15 minutes. Serve immediately with your choice of dressing.

Pinwheel Tortillas

1 bag tortillas
1-8 oz. pkg. cream cheese
16 oz. sour cream
Season-All Seasoned Salt
2 sweet yellow or green bell peppers, diced

Spread the cream cheese on one side of each tortilla. Layer the sour cream and peppers evenly to cover the top. Sprinkle with Season-All. Roll each tortilla and cut into ½-inch slices. Arrange on a plate and serve.

Ranch Flavored Pretzels

¼ tsp. garlic salt

½ tsp. lemon pepper seasoning

1 envelope ranch dressing mix

1 cup vegetable oil

2 lb. small pretzels

In a small bowl, mix the first four ingredients very well. Put the pretzels into a large mixing bowl. Pour the mixture over the pretzels and stir until coated throughout.

Sour Cream and Onion Flavored Pretzels

3 tbsp. sour cream and onion powder

½ tsp. garlic powder

¼ tsp. dried dill weed

1 envelope ranch dressing mix

1 cup vegetable oil

2 lb. small pretzels

Mix the first four ingredients in a small bowl. Add the oil and mix until well blended. Pour the pretzels into a large mixing bowl, add the mixture, and stir well.

Sarah Ann Mae's Soft Pretzels

2 tbsp. butter

½ cup light brown sugar, packed

1 tsp. salt

4 tbsp. powdered yeast

2 cups warm water

4–5 cups flour

2 oz. pretzel salt

Dipping Solution:

2 heaping tbsp. baking soda

3 cups warm water

Melt the butter in a small saucepan and cook until brown. Combine it with the sugar, salt, yeast, and 2 cups of warm water in a large bowl. Slowly add the flour, mixing until it forms a dough. Cover the bowl with plastic wrap and let rise for 15 minutes. Roll out and cut into strips 18 inches long and as big around as a nickel. Next, add the baking soda to the warm water to make the dipping solution. Twist each strip into a pretzel shape, then dip the unbaked pretzel strips into the baking soda solution, one at a time. Sprinkle with pretzel salt, and place on a nonstick cookie sheet. Bake at 500° for 8–10 minutes or until golden brown. Remove pretzels from cookie sheet. Eat warm or cold.

Chocolate-Coated Crackers

1 lb. semisweet chocolate chips

1-16 oz. jar creamy peanut butter

1 box crackers of your choice

candy sprinkles, optional

Melt the chocolate in a double boiler. Spread the peanut butter on half of the crackers and place another cracker on top. Dip each in the melted chocolate. Place on waxed paper to harden. Lightly dash the sprinkles on the tops of the chocolate-coated crackers.

Christmas Pretzels

1 bag small pretzels

1 lb. bag chocolate wafer cookies

1 small bag M&M's

Place the pretzels on cookie sheet a ½ inch apart. Place a chocolate wafer on top of each pretzel. Bake at 350° for 3 minutes or until chocolate is slightly melted, then remove from oven and top with one M&M on each wafer. Cool first, then remove from the cookie sheet.

White Chocolate Party Mix

2-12 oz. pkgs. vanilla chips
3 tbsp. vegetable oil
1-10 oz. pkg. mini pretzels
5 cups Cheerios
5 cups Corn Chex
2 cups salted peanuts
1 lb. M&M's

Melt the vanilla chips in the oil and stir until smooth. Set aside. In a large bowl, combine the rest of the ingredients. Pour the chips mixture over the dry ingredients and mix well. Spread the mixture in a single layer on waxed paper. Let it cool. Break into pieces and store in the refrigerator. This is a great treat for a holiday.

Frozen Cantaloupe

3 cups sugar
2 cups water
1 tsp. apple cider vinegar
4 medium cantaloupes

Mix the sugar, water, and vinegar together. Take the skin off the cantaloupes and cut them into 2-inch cubes. Place the cubes in the syrup and freeze. Thaw for a half hour before serving.

Finger Jell-O

2-6 oz. pkgs. cherry Jell-O (or raspberry)
2½ cups boiling water
1 cup cold milk, pasteurized
1-3.4 oz. pkg. instant vanilla pudding

Dissolve the Jell-O in boiling water. Let stand for a half hour. Then add the cold milk and pudding mix. Stir until blended. Refrigerate for 1 hour. Cut into squares and enjoy.

Jell-O Squares

1-3 oz. pkg. unflavored gelatin
1-3 oz. pkg. Jell-O, any flavor
1 cup boiling water
1 tbsp. lemon juice

Empty both gelatin packages into a medium mixing bowl, add the boiling water, and dissolve completely. Stir in the lemon juice until blended. Chill until set, then cut into squares.

Jigglers

2½ cups boiling water
1⅓ cups Jell-O powder, any flavor
1 cup milk
⅓ cup instant pudding mix

In 9" x 13" baking dish, mix together the water and Jell-O until dissolved. Add the milk and pudding mix and blend well. Chill until firm. Serve.

CHAPTER 3

Dips, Spreads, & Sauces

Fruit Dip

6 oz. marshmallow creme
1-8 oz. pkg. cream cheese
1 tbsp. Jell-O powder, any flavor
fresh fruit

Cream all the ingredients together in a mixing bowl. Chill. Serve with fresh fruit of your choice. Strawberries are highly recommended.

Honey Mustard Dip

1 cup water
1 cup apple cider vinegar
6 eggs
6 tbsp. dry mustard
3 tbsp. honey mustard onion powder
½ tsp. salt
1½ cups sugar
1 tbsp. flour
½ stick butter

Add all the ingredients except the butter. Blend well. Heat until warm throughout then add the butter. Makes 2½ pints. Serve with soft pretzels.

Veggie Dip

16 oz. sour cream
1-8 oz. pkg. cream cheese
3 tbsp. sour cream and onion powder
3 tbsp. cheddar cheese powder
½ cup sugar

Blend all the ingredients very well. Chill. Serve with chips or raw veggies.

Cheese Ball

2-8oz. pkgs. cream cheese
2 cups shredded sharp cheddar cheese
2 tsp. minced onion
1 tsp. lemon juice
1 tsp. dry mustard
2 tsp. Worcestershire sauce
½ tsp. paprika
½ tsp. salt
½ tsp. Season-All Seasoned Salt
1 cup nut pieces of your choice
⅛ cup parsley flakes

Mix the first nine ingredients together. Blend well, then form into a ball. Set aside. Stir the nuts and parsley flakes together and roll cheese ball over mixture until it is all used up. Chill overnight. Serve with crackers or vegetable strips.

Horseradish and Cheddar Cheese Spread

5 lb. American cheese, grated
2 heaping tbsp. cheddar cheese powder
8 oz. prepared horseradish

Mix all the ingredients well and chill overnight. A nice bitey spread that's great with veggies or crackers.

Bar-B-Q Sauce

1 cup vegetable oil

2 cups apple cider vinegar

½ cup water

4 tbsp. salt

1 tsp. black pepper

2 tsp. poultry seasoning

1 tsp. Worcestershire sauce

2 tsp. garlic salt

Mix all the ingredients together. Baste on meat frequently. Great with grilled chicken. Makes enough sauce for ten chicken halves.

Pizza Sauce

10 quarts tomatoes, cut in quarters

10 medium onions, diced

20 stalks celery, chopped

5 cups ketchup

20 tsp. paprika

10 tsp. garlic powder

10 tbsp. parsley flakes

1 gallon tomato paste

20 tsp. salt

10 tsp. dry mustard

10 tsp. oregano

Cook the tomatoes, onions, and celery until tender. Pour through a tomato juicer and press to make juice. Discard the pulp. Add the remaining ingredients to the juice. Cook over medium to medium-high heat until thickened. Serve on pasta.

Salsa

7 cups tomatoes (plum tomatoes, if available), with peel

2 cups diced red or green bell peppers

4 hot (or mild) peppers

½ cup onion

1 large carrot, grated

1 cup tomato paste

½ cup light brown sugar, packed

¼ cup apple cider vinegar

1 tbsp. oregano

1 tbsp. parsley flakes

1 tbsp. basil

1 tbsp. salt

7 or 8 pint jars with lids

Chop the tomatoes, peppers, and onions into small pieces. Add the remaining ingredients and bring to a boil. Reduce heat and simmer for 20 minutes. Cook longer for a thicker salsa.

This recipe may be canned for storage. To cold pack, put the jars in a 7- or 11-quart canner. Fill the canner with water, stopping ½ inch from the top. Bring the water to a boil and continue to boil for 20 minutes. Follow the lid directions on the package. Serve with chips or crackers.

CHAPTER 4

Sandwich & Soups

The Ultimate Grilled Cheese Sandwich

3oz. cream cheese

¾ cup mayonnaise

1 cup cheddar cheese, shredded

1 cup mozzarella cheese, shredded

½ tsp. garlic powder

⅛ tsp. seasoned salt

10 slices of bread

In a medium bowl, mix the cream cheese and mayo until creamy. Stir in the cheddar, mozzarella, garlic powder, and seasoned salt. Butter one side of the bread slices. Spread about ⅓ cup of the mixture on the dry side of five of the slices. Place the remaining slices on top with the buttered side out, to make sandwiches. Fry in a pan, turning once so they are golden brown on both sides.

Cream of Carrot Soup

½ cup chopped onions

2 tbsp. butter (or margarine)

1 lb. (or 8–10) carrots, shredded

1 lb. (or 3–5) potatoes, shredded

1 cup chicken broth

½ tsp. dried thyme

1 bay leaf

⅛ tbsp. Tabasco sauce

½ tsp. sugar

salt to taste

black pepper to taste

water to cover

1½ cups milk

1 cup shredded cheddar cheese

fresh parsley or flakes (optional)

Sauté onions in butter until tender. Set aside. In a large pot, cover the next nine ingredients with water and bring to a boil. Add the milk and heat again. Discard the bay leaf. Turn the burner on low and add the cheese. Stir well until melted. Pour into individual soup bowls and sprinkle with parsley, if desired.

Spaghetti Soup

½ bushel tomatoes, juice only

3 stalks celery

1 lb. butter

4 onions

4 lb. ground beef

3 lb. navy beans

6 tbsp. salt

3 cups light brown sugar, packed

4 tbsp. chili powder

5 carrots, sliced

3 lb. spaghetti

18–20 quart jars with lids

Put the tomatoes through a tomato juicer and press to make juice. Put the juice aside and discard the pulp. Dice the celery and set aside. Brown the butter and add the onions, sautéing until soft. Set aside. Brown the ground beef. Drain off the grease and set aside. Combine the onions, ground beef, celery, beans, tomatoes, salt, brown sugar, chili powder, and carrots. Cook until almost soft. Cook the spaghetti as directed on the box. Drain and add to the soup.

This recipe is great canned. To cold pack, put the jars in a 7- or 11-quart canner. Fill the canner with water, stopping ½ inch from the top. Bring the water to a boil and continue to boil for 10 minutes. Follow the lid directions on the package. Cold pack for 2½ hours.

CHAPTER 5

Salads & Dressings

Angel Salad

1 egg, separated
1 large can crushed pineapple
juice of 1 lemon
2 tbsp. sugar
1 tbsp. flour
1 lb. marshmallows, cut in quarters
1 cup pecans (or walnuts), roughly chopped
1 cup whipping cream

Beat the egg white and set aside. Drain the juice from the pineapple and set aside. In a saucepan, combine the pineapple juice, lemon juice, egg yolk, sugar, and flour. Cook until thickened. Cool. Stir in the marshmallows and crushed pineapple. Add the whipping cream on top. Chill well before serving.

Apple Salad

1 egg
½ cup sugar
½ cup water
1 tbsp. flour
pinch of salt
1 tsp. apple cider vinegar
2 tbsp. butter
1-8 oz. pkg. Cool Whip
8 Red or Golden Delicious apples, diced

Beat the egg, sugar, water, flour, and salt together in a saucepan and bring to a boil. Add the vinegar and butter and cook for another 2 minutes over medium heat. Cool. Fold in the Cool Whip and diced apples. Chill before serving.

Indiana Salad

1-6 oz. pkg. Jell-O, any flavor
4 cups boiling water
1-8 oz. pkg. cream cheese, softened
1-8 oz. pkg. Cool Whip
1½ cups pineapple juice
1 cup sugar
3 egg yolks
3 tbsp. flour
pinch of salt

Dissolve the Jell-O the in boiling water. Pour into two or three individual serving bowls. Chill until firm. Mix the cream cheese and Cool Whip together and blend well. Evenly distribute the cream cheese mixture on top of the Jell-O. Chill again. In a medium saucepan, cook the remaining ingredients until thickened. Chill separately until firm, then spread on top of the Jell-O and cream cheese layers. Serve cold.

Creamy Cole Slaw

1 large head of cabbage, shredded
1 cup celery, diced
2 carrots, shredded
½ green bell pepper, diced

Dressing:
1½ cups salad dressing
1 cup sugar
1 cup Cool Whip
2 tbsp. apple cider vinegar
salt to taste
celery salt to taste

In a large mixing bowl, combine the cabbage, celery, carrots, and green pepper. Set aside. Place the dressing ingredients in another large bowl and mix well. Add the cabbage mixture to the dressing mixture. Chill and serve.

Potato Salad

6 cups cooked potatoes, sliced or grated
6 hard-boiled eggs, sliced or grated
½ cup chopped onions
¾ cup chopped celery
½ lb. bacon, fried and crumbled (optional)

Dressing:
1½ cups mayonnaise
1½ tbsp. honey mustard
1½ tbsp. apple cider vinegar
1½ tsp. salt
¾ cup sugar

Combine the potatoes, eggs, onions, celery, and bacon (if desired) in a bowl and mix gently. Mix dressing ingredients in a separate bowl. Combine and chill for 3 hours or overnight. Serve.

Taco Salad

1 lb. ground beef
1 pkg. taco seasoning
6 taco shells (or flour tortillas)
1 head lettuce, shredded
2 medium tomatoes, diced
1 medium onion, chopped
8 oz. sour cream
8 oz. Cheez Whiz

Brown the beef in a skillet. Drain off the grease. Add the taco seasoning, following the directions on the package. Keep warm on the stove. Meanwhile, wrap the taco shells tightly in foil and bake at 500° for 5–10 minutes. Divide the beef mixture into the taco shells. Add the remaining ingredients in amounts as desired for each shell. Serve immediately.

Creamy Salad Dressing

2 cups mayonnaise

½ cup sugar

1 tbsp. yellow mustard

1 tbsp. apple cider vinegar

¼ tsp. salt

¼ tsp. black pepper

¼ tsp. celery seed

Mix all the ingredients well. Chill. Tastes great on fresh greens with a variety of veggies.

CHAPTER 6

Main Courses & Side Dishes

Barbecued Meatballs

Meat Mixture:

- 2 cups quick oats
- 1 can evaporated milk
- 3 eggs, beaten
- 2 tsp. chili powder
- 2 tsp. salt
- ½ tsp. black pepper
- ½ tsp. garlic powder
- 3 lb. ground beef

Sauce:

- 2 cups ketchup
- 1½ cups light brown sugar, packed
- 2 tbsp. liquid smoke
- ½ tsp. garlic powder
- ½ cup onions, chopped
- parsley flakes (optional)

In a large bowl, combine all of the meat mixture ingredients, except the ground beef, and blend well. Then add the ground beef and mix thoroughly. Shape into bite-size balls. Set aside. In a medium bowl, blend all the sauce ingredients. Place the meatballs in a 9" x 13" baking pan and pour the sauce on top. Bake at 350° for 1 hour.

Cheddar Meat Loaf

3 eggs

¾ cup milk

1 cup shredded cheddar cheese

½ cup quick oats

½ cup onions, chopped

1 tsp. salt

dash of black pepper

1 lb. ground beef

Sauce:

⅔ cup ketchup

½ cup light brown sugar, packed

1½ tsp. yellow mustard

In a mixing bowl, beat the eggs and milk. Stir in the cheese, oats, onions, salt, and pepper. Add the beef and mix thoroughly. Place in a bread baking pan. Mix the ketchup, brown sugar, and mustard to make the sauce. Pour over the meat. Bake uncovered at 350° for 45 minutes.

Chicken Casserole

2 lb. (1 quart) cooked chicken (or turkey)

1 can cream of chicken soup

1 cup sour cream

1 stick butter

1½ cups crushed Ritz Crackers

Cut the meat into bite-size pieces. Place in an 8" x 8" cooking pan. In a small bowl, mix the soup and sour cream together. Pour over the meat. Melt the butter and mix with the crackers. Sprinkle on top and bake at 350° for 40 minutes.

Chicken Lasagna

1 can cream of mushroom soup

1 can cream of chicken soup

1 medium onion, diced

½ cup sour cream

¼ cup mayonnaise

¼ tsp. garlic salt

4 cups chicken, cut in bite-size pieces

1 cup shredded cheddar cheese

1 cup shredded mozzarella cheese

1 box lasagna noodles, cooked

½ cup Parmesan cheese

Mix all the ingredients except the noodles and Parmesan cheese. In a 9" x 13" baking pan, alternate one layer of chicken mixture and one layer of lasagna noodles. Repeat. Top with the Parmesan cheese. Bake at 375° for 45 minutes.

Ham (or Dried Beef) Casserole

1 cup macaroni, uncooked

1 can cream of celery soup (or cream of mushroom soup)

1½ cups milk

1½ cups frozen peas

1¼ lb. ham (or dried beef)

¾ cup Cheez Whiz

3 tbsp. chopped onion

Mix all the ingredients together in a large bowl. Pour into a 9" x 13" baking pan and bake at 350° for 1 hour.

Lazy Wife's Dinner

1 can cream of celery soup (or cream of mushroom soup)

1 cup macaroni, uncooked

1½ cups milk

1½ cups frozen vegetables of your choice

½ lb. Velveeta (or American cheese)

1 cup diced potatoes

1 cup diced carrots

1 cup meat of your choice, cooked and chopped into bite-size pieces

3 tbsp. chopped onion

Mix all the ingredients together and pour into a 9" x 13" baking pan. Bake at 350° for 1½ hours.

Saucy Little Meatballs

Meatballs:

1 lb. ground beef

¾ cup quick oats

1 tsp. salt

¼ tsp. black pepper

1 egg

¾ cup milk

Sauce:

⅓ cup ketchup

1 tbsp. light brown sugar, packed

1 tbsp. dry mustard

Combine all the meatball ingredients, form into bite-size balls, and place them in a baking pan. In a small bowl, mix the ketchup, brown sugar, and mustard to make a sauce. Pour the sauce over the meatballs. Bake at 350° for 1 hour.

Spaghetti

2 lb. ground beef

1 cup minced onion

water to cover

1 lb. spaghetti noodles, cooked

1 tsp. salt

1–1½ quarts tomato juice

1 tsp. oregano

1 tsp. garlic salt

½ cup powdered cheddar cheese

Brown the beef in a skillet, breaking it into small pieces with a spatula. Drain and place the meat in a large saucepan. Add the onion and just enough water to cover. Bring to a boil. Add the noodles and salt, and simmer for a half hour. Add the tomato juice, oregano, and garlic salt, and heat thoroughly. Serve topped with powdered cheddar cheese.

Stromboli

Dough:
1 pkg. active dry yeast

1 cup warm water

1 tsp. sugar

2 tbsp. vegetable oil

2½ cups bread flour

Filling:
1 lb. cheese, diced

½ lb. ham, diced

½ lb. salami, diced

2 tbsp. spaghetti sauce (or cream of mushroom soup)

1 medium onion, diced (optional)

Topping:
1 tsp. seasoned salt

1 tbsp. butter, melted

1-16 oz. jar spaghetti or pizza sauce

In a large bowl, mix all of the dough ingredients. Wait 5 minutes then divide the dough into six equal parts. Roll each into a circle. Each stuffed stromboli will have a top and bottom circle of dough. On three of the circles, place ⅓ of the cheese and meat in the center, making sure to leave an empty edge all around, then add the onion and sauce. Cover each with a plain dough circle. Pinch the edges all around to seal tight. Sprinkle tops with seasoned salt and bake at 350° for 20 minutes. Brush each with the butter, top with sauce, and serve.

Shipwreck

1 quart potatoes, sliced

1 large onion, diced

1 lb. ground beef

¼ cup rice, uncooked

1 small stalk celery, diced

1 small can kidney beans

1½ cup cooked tomatoes, canned or fresh

¼ cup water

2 tsp. salt

¼ tsp. black pepper

In a large casserole dish, layer the first seven ingredients. Pour the water on top and sprinkle with salt and pepper. Cover and bake at 350° for 1½–2 hours.

Cooked Celery for Six

2 quarts celery
1 cup water
1 tsp. salt
4 tbsp. butter
½ cup sugar
2 tsp. apple cider vinegar
½ can evaporated milk
2½ tbsp. light brown sugar, packed
2 tbsp. flour

Wash the celery and trim the ends. Cut into bite-size pieces. Place the celery in a saucepan with the water, salt, and butter, and boil until soft. Add the remaining ingredients and cook until it thickens.

Paprika Potatoes

¼ cup flour
¼ cup Parmesan cheese
1 tbsp. paprika
¾ tsp. salt
⅛ tsp. garlic salt (or onion salt)
6 medium potatoes
vegetable oil

Put all the ingredients, except the potatoes, into a gallon-size plastic baggie. Shake until well blended. Wash the potatoes and cut them into small wedges. Add potato wedges to the bag until ⅓ full. Shake the bag to coat the potatoes. Place them on an oiled pan and repeat until all the potatoes are covered with the mixture. Bake at 350° for 1 hour. Serve with our homemade ketchup.

White Minute Rice

1 cup Minute White Rice
¾ cup sweetened condensed milk
dash of cinnamon

Cook the rice following the package directions. When the rice is done, place it in a mixing bowl and add the condensed milk. Sprinkle the cinnamon on top. Serve in place of noodles.

CHAPTER 7

Breads, Rolls, & Muffins

White Bread

2 tbsp. active dry yeast
¾ cup sugar
4 cups warm water
2 tbsp. shortening
1 tbsp. salt
1 tbsp. apple cider vinegar
10–12 cups flour

Dissolve the yeast and sugar in warm water. Add the shortening, salt, and vinegar and mix well. Mix in the flour slowly until blended. Cover with plastic wrap and let rise until doubled (approximately 1½ hours). Punch down. Let rise again for 30–45 minutes. Divide into five equal parts. Smooth out each loaf and place in its own bread pan. Let rise until 1 inch above sides (about a ½ hour). Bake at 350° for 25–30 minutes.

Cinnamon Sticks

1 loaf of bread

1-8 oz. pkg. cream cheese, softened

1 egg yolk

1¼ cups sugar

1 stick butter

1 tsp. cinnamon

Cut off the crusts on all four sides of the bread. Roll each slice of bread until flat. In a medium bowl, mix the cream cheese, yolk, and ¾ cup sugar. Spread some mixture on each piece of bread and roll it up. In a small mixing bowl, blend the remaining sugar and the cinnamon. Dip bread stick into melted butter. Then roll each bread stick in the mixture and place on a cookie sheet. Bake at 350° for ½ hour.

Bun Cake

1 box yellow cake mix

½ cup sugar

4 eggs

3 tsp. cinnamon

8 oz. sour cream

¾ cup light brown sugar, packed

¾ cup vegetable oil

Glaze:

2½ cups powdered sugar

4–5 tbsp. milk (a little more if needed to spread)

3 tsp. vanilla

In a large mixing bowl, blend all the ingredients until well mixed. Pour into a 9" x 13" baking pan and bake at 350° for 35–40 minutes. When the cake is cool, blend all of the glaze ingredients together and spread on top of the cake. Cut into squares and serve.

Icing Buns

¼ cup lard

1 cup scalded milk

¼ cup sugar

¼ cup warm water

1 heaping tbsp. active dry yeast

3½ cups bread flour

Sugar Mixture:

1 cup light brown sugar, packed

2 tsp. cinnamon

½ cup butter, melted

Mix lard, milk, sugar, water, yeast, and flour together in a large bowl. Cover with plastic wrap and let rise for 2 hours, then roll the dough out to a ¼-inch thickness. In a small bowl, combine the sugar mixture ingredients and sprinkle it evenly on top of the dough. Roll the dough into a long log shape. Cut 2-inch slices and place them close together, sides touching, in a 9" x 13" baking pan. Bake at 350° for 25–30 minutes. Slightly cool to warm, and top with Vanilla Frosting (see page 66) or your own favorite frosting.

Sticky Buns

1 box yellow cake mix

5 cups flour

5 tbsp. active dry yeast

2½ cups hot water

1 cup light brown sugar, packed

½ cup butter

4 heaping tbsp. cinnamon

cooking spray

Brown Sugar Icing:

½ cup butter

1 cup light brown sugar

¼ cup milk

2 cups powdered sugar

In a large mixing bowl, combine the cake mix, flour, and yeast. Stir well. Add the hot water and mix well. Cover with plastic wrap and let rise for 2 hours. Roll out the dough to ¼-inch thickness and sprinkle brown sugar evenly on the top. Cut butter into small pieces and scatter over the top, then sprinkle on the cinnamon. Roll into a long log and cut into ½-inch pieces. Place in a greased pan and let rise until doubled in size. Bake at 350° on a greased cookie sheet for 20 minutes or until golden brown.

In the meantime, melt the butter and brown sugar together and cook over low heat for 2 minutes. Add the milk, stirring constantly until the mixture boils. Remove from the heat and cool. Beat in the powdered sugar until smooth. Spread on warm buns and serve.

Baked French Muffins

5 tbsp. margarine (or butter)

½ cup sugar

1 egg

2½ tsp. baking powder

¼ tsp. salt

½ tsp. nutmeg

1½ cups flour

½ cup milk

Topping:

¼ cup butter, melted

½ tsp. cinnamon

In a large mixing bowl, cream the margarine, sugar, and egg. In another bowl, mix the baking powder, salt, nutmeg, and flour together. Add to the first mixture. Slowly pour in the milk until well blended. Fill a greased muffin pan half full. Bake at 350° for approximately 25 minutes or until the tops are golden and they spring back when lightly tapped. Meanwhile, mix the topping ingredients together. After the muffins are done, remove from the oven and brush with the topping mixture. Serve while hot. Makes 1 dozen.

CHAPTER 8

Cakes & Frostings

U-PICK PUMPKINS $4.00

Angel Food Cake

2 cups egg whites
¾ tsp. salt
1½ tsp. cream of tartar
1½ tsp. vanilla
1 cup sugar
1 cup flour, sifted
1½ cups powdered sugar
2 tbsp. cornstarch

In a mixing bowl, combine the egg whites, salt, cream of tartar, vanilla, sugar, flour, powdered sugar, and cornstarch. Stir well. Pour into a greased cake pan or 9" x 13" baking pan. Bake at 350° for 45 minutes to 1 hour. To test for doneness, a toothpick inserted in the center of the cake should come out clean. Top with the frosting of your choice.

Caramel Fudge Cake

1 box chocolate cake mix
½ cup butter
1-14 oz. pkg. caramels
1 can sweetened condensed milk
1 cup chopped peanuts

Prepare the cake mix batter as directed on the package. Pour 2 cups of the batter into a greased pan. Bake at 350° for 15 minutes. Meanwhile, melt the butter and caramels in a saucepan with the condensed milk, stirring until smooth. Spread evenly over the cake. Spread the remaining batter over the caramel mixture. Top with the nuts, return the pan to the oven, and bake for another 30–35 minutes. Cool and spread with the frosting of your choice.

Carrot Cake

4 eggs, beaten

2 cups sugar

1½ cups vegetable oil

3 cups carrots, grated

2 cups flour

2 tsp. baking soda

pinch of salt

Cream Cheese Frosting:

1-8 oz. pkg. cream cheese, softened

1½ cups powdered sugar

1 tsp. grated lemon peel

1 tbsp. lemon juice

In a mixing bowl, combine all the ingredients until well blended. Pour into a Bundt pan. Bake at 350° for 50 minutes or when toothpick inserted in the cake comes out clean. Combine the frosting ingredients and beat until smooth. Spread on the cake after it has cooled.

Cheesecake

Filling:

1-8 oz. pkg. cream cheese, softened

1 cup sugar

1-14 oz. can evaporated milk, chilled

2 tsp. vanilla

1-3 oz. pkg. Jell-O, any flavor

Crust:

32 graham crackers, crushed

1 stick butter, melted

½ cup sugar

In a medium bowl, blend the cream cheese and sugar. Stir in the milk and vanilla. Add the powdered Jell-O and mix again. Set aside. In a medium bowl, mix all of the crust ingredients. Press the graham cracker mixture evenly on the bottom and sides of a pie tin. Pour in the cream cheese mixture and refrigerate until completely chilled.

Cherry Cheesecake

1 box white cake mix

2-8 oz. pkgs. cream cheese, softened

4 cups powdered sugar

2-8 oz. pkgs. Cool Whip

2 cans cherry pie filling

Prepare the cake mix as directed on the box. Bake in a 9" x 13" baking pan, or two pans for a thinner cake. While the cake is baking, beat the cream cheese and sugar until fluffy then fold in the Cool Whip. Cool the cake and spread the mixture over the top and the sides. Top with the pie filling.

Coffee Cake

Batter:

1 box yellow cake mix

1-4 oz. pkg. vanilla instant pudding

2 tbsp. vegetable oil

1⅓ cups water

2 eggs

Topping:

½ cup flour

½ cup light brown sugar, packed

2 tbsp. melted butter

2 tsp. cinnamon

In a large mixing bowl, beat the batter ingredients together. Set aside. In another mixing bowl, mix the topping ingredients. Pour half the batter into a 9" x 13" baking pan. Cover with half the topping mixture. Repeat. Bake at 350° for 35–38 minutes. Cool and serve.

Cream Cheese Cupcakes

Batter:
- 3-8 oz. pkgs. cream cheese
- 5 eggs
- 1 cup flour
- 1½ tsp. vanilla

Frosting:
- 1 cup sour cream
- 1 tsp. vanilla
- ¼ cup sugar
- 1 can pie filling (cherry, blueberry, or peach)

Combine all the batter ingredients together and mix well. Line cupcake pan with cupcake papers and fill them ⅔ full. Bake at 300° for 40 minutes. Meanwhile, in a small bowl, mix together the ingredients for the frosting. When the cupcakes are done, remove the pan from the oven and cool for 5 minutes. Spoon the frosting on top of the cupcakes and bake for another 5 minutes. Cool in pan.

Éclair Cake

Batter:
- 6 cups milk
- 6 egg yolks
- 3 heaping tbsp. cornstarch
- 3 heaping tbsp. flour
- 1 cup light brown sugar, packed
- 1-8 oz. pkg. Cool Whip

Crust:
- 2 cups graham cracker crumbs

Icing:
- 2 tbsp. vegetable oil
- 3 tbsp. unsweetened cocoa powder
- 2 tsp. light corn syrup
- 2 tsp. vanilla
- 3 tbsp. butter
- 3 tbsp. milk
- 1½ cups powdered sugar

In a large mixing bowl, mix all the batter ingredients except the Cool Whip. Cook over medium heat until the mixture thickens. Cool. Fold in the Cool Whip. Pour half the batter into a 9" x 13" baking pan. Then place a layer of whole graham crackers on top. Repeat. Combine the icing ingredients, blend until smooth, and spread on top. Chill again.

German Apple Cake

1 cup sour milk	2 eggs
1 tsp. apple cider vinegar	2¼ cups flour
2 tsp. baking soda	¼ tsp. salt
½ cup vegetable oil	1½ cinnamon
¾ cup sugar	2 cups apples, peeled
½ cup light brown sugar, packed	and diced

Topping:
½ cup light brown sugar, packed
¼ cup sugar
½ tsp. cinnamon

Add the vinegar to the milk to make sour milk. Stir in the baking soda. Place the oil in a large bowl and add the sugar, brown sugar, eggs, flour, salt, cinnamon, sour milk mixture, and apples, in that order. Pour into a 9" x 13" baking pan. In a small bowl, mix all the topping ingredients together. Sprinkle topping on the batter. Bake at 350° for 35–40 minutes.

Mini Cheesecakes

2-8 oz. pkgs. cream cheese
1 tsp. vanilla
½ cup sugar
2 eggs
12 vanilla wafers
1 can pie filling (fruit of your choice)

In a mixing bowl, beat the cream cheese, vanilla, and sugar together. Add the eggs and mix well. Place one wafer in each muffin cup in a nonstick muffin pan. Pour the batter into each cup until half full. Bake at 325° for 25 minutes. Cool. Spread pie filling on top.

Shoofly Cake

Syrup:	**Crumbs:**
3 eggs	3 cups flour
1 cup light brown sugar, packed	2 cups light brown sugar, packed
1 tsp. vanilla	½ tsp. salt
1 cup molasses	pinch of cream of tartar
1½ cups hot water	pinch of cinnamon
	1 stick margarine, softened

In a medium bowl, combine all the syrup ingredients and mix well. Set aside. Blend all the crumb ingredients together in a mixing bowl. Add 4 cups of the crumb mixture to the syrup and stir for about 2 minutes. Place in a 9" x 13" baking pan and top with the remaining crumb mixture. Bake at 375° for 40 minutes or until the top is slightly golden brown.

Sour Cream Cheesecake

1 lb. small curd cottage cheese

2-8 oz. pkgs. cream cheese, softened

1½ cups sugar	2 tbsp. lemon juice
4 eggs	1 tsp. vanilla
⅓ cup cornstarch	½ cup butter, melted
1 pint sour cream	1 graham cracker crust (ready-made)

In a large mixing bowl, blend the cottage cheese and cream cheese until creamy. Except for the crust, beat in the remaining ingredients until well blended. Pour the batter into the graham cracker crust. Bake at 325° for about 60–70 minutes or until the edges are firm. Turn off the oven. Leave the cake in the oven for 2 more hours. Remove and chill in the refrigerator.

Strawberry Shortcake

½ cup butter
1 cup sugar
2 eggs
¾ tsp. vanilla
½ cup milk

1¾ cup flour
¼ tsp. salt
3 tbsp. baking powder
1 quart strawberries; sliced

In a mixing bowl, combine the butter, sugar, eggs, vanilla, and milk. Blend well. In another bowl, sift the flour, salt, and baking powder together. Add to the first mixture. Pour the batter into a buttered baking pan and bake at 350° for 40 minutes. Cool and add strawberries on top.

Wet Bottom Shoofly Cake

Wet Bottom:
3 cups light brown sugar, packed
1½ cups molasses
3 cups hot water
4 eggs

Crumb Topping:
1 cup light brown sugar, packed
6 cups flour
1½ tsp. baking soda
1 tsp. salt
1 tsp. cream of tartar
1 cup lard

In a mixing bowl, combine all the wet bottom ingredients and pour into two nonstick 9" x 13" baking pans. In another bowl, blend the crumb topping ingredients. Spread the crumb topping over the wet bottom in each pan. Bake at 400° for 15 minutes. Reduce oven temperature to 350° and bake 25 minutes longer. Cool to serve.

Zucchini Cake

3 eggs, beaten

2 cups sugar

2 tbsp. vanilla

2 cups zucchini, grated

1 cup vegetable oil

3 cups flour

1 tsp. baking powder

1 tsp. baking soda

1 tsp. salt

1 cup crushed pineapple, packed in juice

1 cup raisins

Glaze:

3 oz. cream cheese, softened

⅓ cup butter (or margarine)

2 cups powdered sugar

1 tsp. vanilla

In a large mixing bowl, combine all the batter ingredients, except the raisins. In a saucepan, boil the raisins, drain, then add to the batter. Blend well. Pour the batter into a 9" x 13" baking pan. Bake at 325° for 1 hour. Cool. For the glaze, mix together the cream cheese and butter and blend well. Gradually add the powdered sugar then the vanilla. Spread on the cake after it has cooled.

Chocolate Icing

¼ cup butter (or margarine), melted

½ cup unsweetened cocoa powder

¼ tsp salt

⅓ cup milk

1½ tsp. vanilla

3½ cups powdered sugar

In a mixing bowl, blend the butter, cocoa, and salt together. Add the milk, vanilla, and powdered sugar. Mix thoroughly until creamy.

Vanilla Frosting

2 tbsp. flour

1 cup milk

¼ cup butter

1 cup sugar

1 tbsp. vanilla

½ cup shortening

Heat the flour and milk in a saucepan until thickened. Cool. Add the remaining ingredients, beating until the frosting is fluffy.

CHAPTER 9

Desserts, Puddings, & Pies

Apple Goodie

Bottom:
- 1½ cups sugar
- 2 tbsp. flour
- pinch of salt
- 1 tsp. cinnamon
- 1½ quarts apples, sliced

Top:
- 1 cup quick oats
- 1 cup sugar
- 1 cup flour
- ¼ tsp. baking soda
- ⅓ tsp. baking powder
- ⅔ cup butter

In a large mixing bowl, combine the first four bottom mixture ingredients. Add to the sliced apples and mix. Pour into two greased 9" x 13" baking pans. In another bowl, blend all the ingredients for the top mixture until crumbly. Add to the pans and press firmly. Bake at 350° for 25 minutes or until golden brown. Serve warm with Homemade Vanilla Ice Cream (see page 72).

Berry Fluff

Crust:
- 2 cups graham cracker crumbs
- 5 tbsp. butter, melted

Top Layer:
- 2 egg whites
- 1 tbsp. vanilla
- 1½ cups sugar
- 2 cups berries of choice
- 1-8 oz. pkg. Cool Whip

Mix the graham cracker crumbs and butter, and press on bottom and sides of a 9" x 13" baking pan. Set aside. In a bowl, beat the egg whites and vanilla until almost smooth. Beat in the sugar. Fold in the berries and Cool Whip. Place mixture on top of the graham cracker crust. Freeze before serving and keep frozen until gone.

Christmas Delight

Bottom Layer:
⅓ cup cold water
1-3 oz. pkg. lime Jell-O

Top Layer:
½ cup sugar	1 tsp. vanilla
¾ cup milk	1 can pineapple tidbits, drained
2 egg yolks	2 egg whites
1-3 oz. pkg. lime Jell-O	1 cup Cool Whip

Pour the water into a large bowl. Stir in one package of Jell-O and refrigerate. In a small saucepan, combine the sugar, milk, and egg yolks. Cook until warm, stirring constantly. Remove from the heat and stir in the remaining package of Jell-O and the vanilla. Add the pineapple, blend well, and store in the refrigerator until it begins to thicken. Beat the egg whites until stiff and fold into the mixture. Add the Cool Whip. Mix well. Spread on top of the first layer. Spoon to serve.

Fluffy Mint Dessert

40 Oreos, crushed
½ cup butter (or margarine)
2-12 oz. pkgs. Cool Whip
2 cups pastel mini marshmallows
1⅓ cups small pastel mints

Set aside ¼ cup of the crushed cookies. In a large mixing bowl, combine the remaining crushed cookies with the butter. Press into a 9" x 13" baking dish. Blend the Cool Whip, marshmallows, and mints. Spread over the entire crust. Top with the remaining ¼ cup of crushed cookies. Refrigerate for 2 hours. Cut into squares and serve.

Fruit Dessert

7 cups water

1 pkg. orange Kool-Aid

1 cup sugar

¾ cup Clear Jel

1 cup water

½ cup orange Jell-O powder

Fruit (or use fruit in season):

2 Red or Golden Delicious apples, peeled and diced

1 can pineapple tidbits in its own juice

2 oranges, sectioned

1 banana, sliced

In a large pot, heat the 7 cups of water to boiling. Add the Kool-Aid and sugar, and continue boiling. Add the Clear Jel and 1 more cup of water. Cook until thick then stir in Jell-O until blended. Cool until partially thickened. Add the apples, pineapple chunks, orange slices, and bananas (or any preferred fruit in season). Chill thoroughly.

ruit Pizza

1½ cups flour

1 cup powdered sugar

¾ cup cold butter (or margarine)

2-8 oz. pkgs. cream cheese

1½ tsp. vanilla

1½ cups whipped cream

fresh fruit of your choice (pineapple, mandarin oranges, strawberries, grapes, bananas)

1 cup pineapple juice

½ cup sugar

2 tbsp. cornstarch

Mix the flour, ½ cup powdered sugar, and the butter. Pat the mixture onto a nonstick pizza pan or in a 9" x 13" baking dish. Bake at 350° for 20–30 minutes. Meanwhile, whip the cream cheese with the remaining ½ cup powdered sugar. Add the vanilla and the whipped cream. Spread on the cooled crust. Top the crust with the fruit of your choice. Cook the pineapple juice, sugar, and cornstarch until clear. Cool at room temperature and drizzle over the fruit. Chill thoroughly.

Homemade Vanilla Ice Cream

4 eggs

¾ cup sugar

⅛ tsp. salt

3 tbsp. vanilla

1 can sweetened condensed milk

3 cups homogenized milk

1½ pints heavy whipping cream

Beat the eggs for 2 minutes. Add the sugar and salt. Beat until creamy. Add the vanilla, sweetened condensed milk, and homogenized milk. Beat until well blended. With a big spoon, stir in the whipping cream. Freeze.

Upside-Down Sundae

2 cups semisweet chocolate chips

1 can evaporated milk

½ tsp. salt

12 oz. vanilla wafers, crushed

½ cup butter, melted

2 quarts ice cream, any flavor

In a saucepan, melt the chocolate chips with the milk and salt. Cook about 20 minutes or until thickened. Set aside. Combine the wafer crumbs with the butter. Set aside 1 cup of the crumb mixture. Press the remaining crumb mixture into a 9" x 13" baking pan and chill for 10 minutes. Pour the chocolate mixture over the crumbs. Cover and freeze until firm. Spread the ice cream over the chocolate. Place the remaining crumb mixture on top. Freeze for another 2 hours. Scoop to serve.

Lemon Delight

1 cup flour
1 stick butter, melted
1-8 oz. pkg. cream cheese
1 cup powdered sugar
1-8 oz. pkg. Cool Whip
3 cups milk
1-4 oz. pkg. lemon pudding

In a mixing bowl, combine the flour and butter. Spread in two 9" x 13" baking pans. Bake at 350° for 15 minutes or until a light golden brown. In another bowl, combine the remaining ingredients and blend well. Pour this mixture on top of the baked crusts. Chill.

Old-Fashioned Apple Crisp

8 large apples (Delicious, or your favorite)
1 tsp. cinnamon
1 cup light brown sugar, packed
1 cup sugar
1 tsp. baking powder
1 cup flour
1 egg
½ tsp. salt
½ cup butter, melted

Grease a 9" x 13" baking dish. Peel and slice apples and place them in the baking dish. Mix the cinnamon with the brown sugar. Sprinkle half the mixture over the apples. In another bowl, combine the sugar, baking powder, flour, egg, and salt. Spread this mixture over the apples. Sprinkle the remaining cinnamon and brown sugar mixture on top. Pour on the melted butter evenly. Bake at 350° for 45 minutes.

Oreo Cookie Dessert

30 Oreo cookies, crumbled

1-8 oz. pkg. cream cheese

¾ cup smooth peanut butter

1 cup milk

2 cups powdered sugar

1-8 oz. pkg. Cool Whip

Set aside ¾ cup of the cookie crumbs for the topping. Spread the remaining broken cookies in a 9" x 13" baking pan. In a mixing bowl, blend the next four ingredients. Pour on top of the crust. Top with the Cool Whip and sprinkle on the remaining cookie crumbs.

Rainbow Jell-O

7-3 oz. pkgs. Jell-O, mixed flavors

1 pint sour cream

7 cups boiling water (1 cup at a time)

3⅔ cups cold water (½ cup at a time)

Dissolve one package of Jell-O in 1 cup boiling water. Divide in half. Add ½ cup cold water to one of the halves. Pour into a clear bowl or pan. Chill until set. Add remaining mixed Jell-O to ⅓ cup sour cream and blend well. Pour on top of the chilled layer. Chill until set. Repeat with the remaining layers. For the top layer, dissolve the Jell-O in 1 cup of boiling water and ⅔ cup cold water. Cool. Pour on top and chill well again.

Caramel Pudding

½ cup light brown sugar, packed
3 tbsp. water
1 tbsp. butter
¼ tsp. baking soda
½ tsp. salt
¼ cup sugar
1 egg
½ cup flour
4 cups milk
1 cup Cool Whip

In a saucepan, combine the brown sugar, water, and butter. Bring to a boil. Add the baking soda and salt, and bring to another boil over medium heat. Add the remaining ingredients except the Cool Whip. Stir until the mixture is thick and syrupy. Pour into individual dessert dishes and cool. Top with Cool Whip and serve.

Egg Custard

4 eggs
3 cups milk
½ cup sugar
1 tsp. vanilla
pinch of salt
sprinkle of cinnamon

Blend the first five ingredients well. Pour into mugs and sprinkle with the cinnamon. Place in a water bath in a saucepan and boil 3 minutes. Chill. Custard will thicken when chilled.

Hot Fudge Pudding

Sauce:
- 2 lb. butter
- ¾ cup white flour
- ¼ cup chocolate syrup
- ½ tsp. salt
- 1⅔ cups water

Batter:
- 1 cup flour
- ¾ cup sugar
- ½ cup milk
- 1 tsp. baking powder
- 1 tbsp. butter, melted
- 2 tbsp. unsweetened cocoa powder

Combine all the sauce ingredients in a saucepan. Boil for 5 minutes, stirring constantly. Pour into two 9" x 13" baking dishes. Mix the batter ingredients and drop by tablespoonfuls onto the sauce in both dishes. Bake at 350° for 30–40 minutes. Great when served hot with ice cream.

Tapioca Pudding

- 1 quart milk, warmed
- ⅓ cup mini tapioca
- 4 egg yolks
- 1 cup sugar
- 1 tsp. vanilla
- 2 heaping tbsp. cornstarch

Pour the milk and tapioca into a medium saucepan and simmer for 20 minutes (do not let it come to a boil). Beat the egg yolks, sugar, and vanilla until thick and creamy. Add to the tapioca mixture after it has simmered and bring it almost to a boil. Add the cornstarch. Stir well. Serve warm or cold.

Chocolate Shoofly Pie

Bottom:

    5 cups sugar

    5 heaping tbsp. cornstarch

    5 heaping tbsp. flour

    5 scant tbsp. unsweetened cocoa powder

    ¼ cup butter

    5 eggs

    5 cups water

    1 tbsp. vanilla

Top:

    2 cups light brown sugar, packed

    1 cup lard

    2 eggs

    2 cups King Syrup

    2 cups hot water

    2 tsp. vanilla

    4½ cups flour

    2 tsp. baking soda

    ½ cup unsweetened cocoa powder

    7 pie pans

Prepare the bottom first. In large mixing bowl, combine all the ingredients in order and cook over medium heat until completely warmed. Cool.

In a large mixing bowl, combine the brown sugar, lard, and eggs, and beat until well blended. Add the remaining top layer ingredients and stir. Divide the cooled bottom mixture evenly into the 7 pie pans. Cover evenly with the top layer mixture. Bake at 350° for 45–55 minutes. Cool and frost with Chocolate Icing (see page 66) or Vanilla Frosting (see page 66). Can be frozen.

Fresh Peach Pie

3 cups water

2¼ cups flour

3 tbsp. Clear Jel

1-9 oz. pkg. orange Jell-O

8 cups peaches, sliced

4 or 5 piecrusts (or graham cracker crusts), ready-made

Bake the piecrusts following package directions. Place the water in a saucepan and add the flour and Clear Jel. Cook over medium heat until clear. Remove from heat and add the Jell-O. Mix well. Cool. Add the peaches and pour into piecrusts. Chill until set.

Fresh Strawberry Pie

Crust:
   1½ cups flour

   ½ tsp. salt

   2 tbsp. milk

   2 tbsp. sugar

   ½ cup vegetable oil

Filling:
   4 oz. cream cheese (double, if desired)

   ½ cup powdered sugar (double, if the cream cheese is doubled)

Strawberry Glaze:
   2 cups water

   1 cup sugar

   1 tsp. vanilla

   ½ tsp. salt

   1-3 oz. pkg. strawberry Jell-O

   1 tbsp. lemon juice

   1 pkg. Clear Jel

   1 quart strawberries

   1-12 oz. pkg. (1½ cups) Cool Whip

Mix the crust ingredients and press into a 9" baking pan. Bake at 425° for 10–15 minutes, or until the crust is a light golden brown. Meanwhile, mix the cream cheese with the powdered sugar. Spread the filling on top of the cooled crust. In a medium saucepan, combine all the glaze ingredients except the strawberries and Cool Whip, and mix well. Cook over medium heat until thickened. Add the strawberries and continue to heat until warm. Pour onto the crust. Chill thoroughly. Top with Cool Whip and serve.

Ice Cream Pie

1½ cups (approximately 30) crushed vanilla wafers (or Ritz Crackers)

1 stick butter, melted

1 quart coffee (or vanilla) ice cream, slightly softened (or Homemade Vanilla Ice Cream, page 72)

3–4 Snickers bars, crushed

1 cup caramel ice cream topping

Mix the crushed wafers with the butter and chill for 15 minutes in a pie pan. Spoon the ice cream onto the crust. Top with crushed Snickers bar. Freeze. Cut into squares. When ready to serve, pour caramel topping over each. Caramel sauce can also be drizzled on before freezing.

Peanut Butter Pie

Filling:

1-8 oz. pkg. cream cheese

1 cup powdered sugar

½ cup creamy peanut butter

1-8 oz. pkg. Cool Whip

Crust:

1½ cups graham cracker crumbs

1 stick butter

3 tbsp. light brown sugar, packed

Blend the first three filling ingredients. Stir in the Cool Whip and set aside. In another bowl, blend the crust ingredients. Press into a 9-inch pie pan. Pour the filling into the crust and chill thoroughly.

Pumpkin Pie

French Piecrust:
- 1½ cups flour
- 2 tbsp. sugar
- ½ cup vegetable oil
- ½ tsp. salt
- 2 tbsp. milk

Filling:
- 2 tbsp. butter
- 2 eggs, separated
- 1 cup canned pumpkin
- ½ cup sugar
- ½ cup light brown sugar, packed
- ½ cup King Syrup
- 2 tbsp. flour
- ½ tsp. cinnamon
- ⅛ tsp. pumpkin pie spice
- ⅛ tsp. salt
- 2 cups milk, warmed
- 1-12 oz. pkg. Cool Whip

This recipe makes 2 pies. Blend the piecrust ingredients in a medium mixing bowl. Divide the dough into two equal parts and press into two 8-inch pie tins. Bake at 400° for 18–20 minutes, or until light golden brown.

Brown the butter in a small saucepan. Set aside. Mix the yolks into the pumpkin. Combine the pumpkin mixture with the remaining filling ingredients, adding the egg whites last. Mix well. Divide the mixture in half and pour into crusts. Bake at 400° for 10 minutes. Lower the temperature to 350° and bake 30 minutes longer. Serve warm or cold. Top with Cool Whip.

CHAPTER 10

Cookies &
Bars

Chocolate Chip Cookies

3 cups butter

2¼ cups light brown sugar, packed

2¼ cups sugar

6 eggs

3 tsp. vanilla

6¾ cups unsifted flour

3 tsp. baking soda

1½ tsp. salt

3 cups chopped nuts

1-12 oz. pkg. Hershey's semisweet chocolate chips

In a large mixing bowl, cream the butter with both sugars, the eggs, and the vanilla until fluffy. In a separate bowl, mix the flour, baking soda, and salt until well blended. Add to the first mixture and stir until mixed well. Stir in the nuts and mix again. On a nonstick or greased cookie sheet, drop the mixture by teaspoonfuls, 1 inch apart. Bake at 375° for 8–10 minutes or until the tops are a light golden brown. Cool slightly before removing from pan.

Chocolate Chip Pudding Cookies

4½ cups flour

2 tsp. baking soda

2 cups butter, softened

½ cup sugar

1½ cups light brown sugar, packed

2-3.4 oz. pkgs. instant vanilla pudding

2 tsp. vanilla

4 eggs, beaten

2-12 oz. bags chocolate chips

In a large bowl, mix all the ingredients, adding the chocolate chips last. Drop onto greased or nonstick cookie sheets. Bake at 350° for 10–12 minutes. Remove from the cookie sheets while still warm.

Chocolate Mint Cookies

½ cup margarine

¼ cup unsweetened cocoa powder

1 cup sugar

1¼ cups flour

1 egg

pinch of salt

½ tsp. baking soda

1 tsp. vanilla

Icing:

1 cup powdered sugar

2 tbsp. butter

1 tsp. peppermint extract

2 tbsp. cream

Place all the cookie ingredients in a large mixing bowl and stir well. Form tablespoons of dough into balls and flatten on cookie sheets. Bake at 350° for approximately 10 minutes. Cool.

Meanwhile, combine icing ingredients in a small bowl, mixing until smooth. Coat cookies with icing.

Ginger Snaps

1 cup sugar

1 cup dark molasses

1 cup lard

1 egg

1 tsp. ground ginger

½ tsp. cinnamon

1 tsp. baking soda

4–5 cups flour

Warm the sugar, molasses, and lard in a saucepan. Stir frequently to cool. Add the egg and blend well. Combine the ginger, cinnamon, baking soda, and just enough flour to make a stiff dough. Mix well. Roll out the dough to a ⅛-inch thickness. Form teaspoons of dough into balls and flatten on cookie sheets. Bake at 350° for 8–10 minutes.

Glazed Apple Cookies

2½ cups light brown sugar, packed

1 cup shortening

2 eggs

4 cups flour

2 tsp. baking soda

1 tsp. salt

2 tsp. ground cloves

1 tsp. nutmeg

2 tsp. cinnamon

½ cup apple juice (or milk)

1 cup nuts

2 cups raisins

2 cups apples, peeled and diced (Jonathan or Red Rome)

Glaze:

3 cups powdered sugar

5 tbsp. (or more) apple juice (or milk)

1 tsp. vanilla

1 tbsp. butter, softened

In a large mixing bowl, combine the sugar, shortening, and eggs. Mix well. In a separate bowl, mix the flour, baking soda, salt, cloves, nutmeg, and cinnamon. Add to the first mixture and blend well. Pour in the apple juice and mix. Blend in the nuts, raisins, and apples. Drop by heaping teaspoonfuls, about 2 inches apart, onto cookie sheets. Bake at 400° for 8 minutes, or until a light golden brown. While the cookies cool, mix the glaze ingredients until blended. Spread on top of the cookies.

Irresistible Peanut Butter Cookies

1½ cups creamy peanut butter

1 cup shortening

2½ cups light brown sugar, packed

6 tbsp. milk

2 tbsp. vanilla

2 eggs

3½ cups flour

1½ tsp. salt

1½ tsp. baking soda

1-12 oz. bag chocolate chips

In a large mixing bowl, blend all the ingredients in the order they are listed. Be sure to add the flour slowly, mixing well after each addition. Drop by heaping teaspoonfuls onto a nonstick cookie sheet. Bake at 350° for 7–8 minutes or until the cookies are a golden brown. Cool.

Molasses Sugar Cookies

½ cup Brer Rabbi molasses

4½ cups shortening

2 eggs, beaten

1½ cups light brown sugar, packed

2 tsp. baking soda

¼ tsp. ground cloves

2 tsp. cinnamon

pinch of salt

4½ cups flour

½ cup sugar

In a large mixing bowl, stir together the molasses, shortening, eggs, and brown sugar. In a separate bowl, combine the baking soda, cloves, cinnamon, salt, and flour until well mixed. Form into bite-size balls and roll them in the sugar. Place on a cookie sheet and bake at 350° for 10 minutes.

No-Bake High Fiber Balls

1 cup creamy peanut butter
1 cup honey
1 cup raisins
1 cup chocolate chips
1 cup sweetened coconut
½ cup bran
3 cups quick oats
¼ tsp. salt

Stir all the ingredients together in a large mixing bowl. Form into bite-size balls and freeze.

Peanut Butter Blossoms

1 cup flour
1 cup light brown sugar, packed
1 cup margarine
1 cup creamy peanut butter
2 eggs
½ tsp. salt
1 tsp. baking soda
3½ cups flour
½ cup milk
1 bag Hershey's Kisses

In a large mixing bowl, combine all ingredients except the Hershey's Kisses. Drop by heaping teaspoonfuls onto a nonstick cookie sheet. Bake at 350° for 6 minutes. Remove from the oven. Place a Hershey's Kiss in the center of each cookie and return to the oven for another 1 or 2 minutes. Cool.

Peanut Butter Chocolate Chip Cookies

¾ cup light brown sugar, packed

½ cup sugar

2 eggs

¾ cup (1½ sticks) margarine

1 tsp. vanilla

¾ cup creamy peanut butter

¾ tsp. baking soda

2½ cups flour

1¾ cups (8 oz.) chocolate chips

In a large bowl, combine the sugars, eggs, and margarine. Add the vanilla and peanut butter and blend well. Mix the baking soda and flour in a separate bowl. Add to the batter and stir until well blended. Pour in chocolate chips and mix thoroughly. Roll into bite-size balls and place on a cookie sheet 2 inches apart. Flatten with a fork, creating a crisscross pattern on top. Bake at 375° for 10 minutes. Cool.

Peanut Butter Cup Cookies

40 mini peanut butter cups

½ cup butter, softened

½ cup light brown sugar, packed

1 egg

½ tsp. vanilla

2¼ cups flour

¾ tsp. salt

1 tsp. baking soda

Unwrap the peanut butter cups and set aside. Blend the remaining ingredients in a large bowl. Roll the dough into small balls and place in mini muffin pans. Bake at 350° for 8–10 minutes until lightly browned. Press one peanut butter cup into the top of each cookie and cool.

Peanut Butter Sandwich Cookies

1 cup butter-flavored shortening

1 cup creamy peanut butter

1 cup sugar

1 cup light brown sugar, packed

1 tsp. vanilla

3 eggs

3 cups flour

¼ tsp. salt

2 tsp. baking soda

Filling:

½ cup butter, softened

1 tsp. vanilla

3 cups powdered sugar

5 tbsp. (or more) milk

In a large mixing bowl, mix together the shortening, peanut butter, and sugars. Add the vanilla and eggs. Beat well. In a separate bowl, sift together the flour, salt, and baking soda. Add to the first mixture and blend well. Shape into bite-size balls. Place on a nonstick cookie sheet. Bake at 375° for 7–8 minutes. Cool.

Meanwhile, blend the filling ingredients in a medium bowl. Spread the filling on the bottom of one cookie and make a sandwich using a second cookie. Repeat until all the cookies are used.

Pumpkin Cookies

2 cups light brown sugar, packed

1 cup vegetable oil

1½ cups pumpkin

3 cups flour

2 eggs, beaten

1 tsp. salt

1 tsp. baking powder

1 tsp. baking soda

1 tsp. vanilla

1½ tbsp. cinnamon

½ tbsp. ground ginger

½ tbsp. ground cloves

Caramel Icing:

½ cup butter

1 cup light brown sugar, packed

¼ cup evaporated milk (or regular milk)

pinch of salt

1¾–2 cups powdered sugar, as needed

Cream the brown sugar and oil together. Add the rest of the ingredients and stir until well blended. Drop by tablespoonfuls onto a nonstick cookie sheet. Bake at 350° for 10 minutes. Remove from the oven and test to see if the cookies are done. If not, return to the oven for an additional 2 minutes. In the meantime, melt the butter for the icing in a saucepan. Add the brown sugar and boil over low heat for 2 minutes, stirring constantly. Mix in the milk and salt. Keep stirring until the mixture comes to a full boil. Remove from the heat and cool to lukewarm. Gradually beat in the powdered sugar to reach a spreadable consistency. Frost the cookies after they have cooled.

Raisin Puffs

1 cup water
1½ cups raisins
1 cup butter
1 tsp. vanilla
2 eggs
1½ cups sugar
3½ cups flour
½ tsp. salt

Topping:
2 tsp. cinnamon
½ cup sugar

Place the water in a saucepan and add the raisins. Boil until the water is gone. Reduce the heat to medium and add the butter. Then add the vanilla, eggs, and sugar in order. Heat completely. Remove from the heat and transfer to a mixing bowl. Mix in the flour and salt. Chill, then mix and form into bite-size balls. Stir cinnamon and sugar together and roll the balls in the topping to cover. Place about 2 inches apart on a nonstick cookie sheet and bake at 350° for 12 minutes. For softer cookies, bake for about 8 minutes.

Sugar Cookies

4 cups light brown sugar, packed

2 cups vegetable oil

8 eggs, unbeaten

4 tsp. baking soda

2 tsp. baking powder

½ tsp. salt

2 tsp. vanilla

1 can evaporated milk

8 cups flour

Sugar Topping:

¼ cup sugar

¼ cup light brown sugar, packed

Combine the sugar, oil, and eggs in a large bowl and mix well. In a small bowl, sift together the baking soda, baking powder, and salt. Add the vanilla and milk. Stir until well blended. Add the flour slowly, blending well after each addition. Drop by teaspoonfuls onto a nonstick cookie sheet, 2 inches apart. Bake at 350° for 8–10 minutes. Cool. Mix the topping in a small bowl and sprinkle over the cookies.

Original Whoopee Pies

1½ cups vegetable oil

3 cups light brown sugar, packed

6 eggs

3 tsp. vanilla

1½ cups milk

3 tsp. baking soda

1½ tsp. salt

1½ tsp. unsweetened cocoa powder

6 cups flour

1 can frosting of choice (or see Index for homemade frostings)

Cream together the oil, sugar, eggs, and vanilla until well blended. Add the milk and mix well. Set aside. Stir together the baking soda, salt, cocoa, and flour in a separate bowl. Add to the first mixture and mix well. Drop by tablespoonfuls onto a nonstick cookie sheet. Bake at 350° for 10 minutes. Cool. Spread the frosting on one side of a pie and place another pie on top to form a sandwich cookie. Repeat for the remaining cookies.

Chocolate Chip Whoopee Pies

2 cups light brown sugar, packed

¾ cup butter

3 eggs

1 tsp. vanilla

1 cup milk

1 tsp. salt

4 cups flour

1 lb. mini chocolate chips

1 can vanilla frosting (or homemade Fluffy Vanilla Frosting, see page 97)

Combine the first seven ingredients in a large mixing bowl. Blend well. Stir in the chocolate chips and mix well. Drop batter by teaspoonfuls onto a nonstick cookie sheet. Bake at 350° for 10–12 minutes. Cool. Spread the frosting on one side of a pie and place another pie on top to form a sandwich cookie. Repeat for the remaining cookies. Can be frozen.

Pumpkin Whoopee Pies

6 cups light brown sugar, packed

3 cups vegetable oil

6 cups pumpkin

6 eggs

3 tsp. cinnamon

3 tsp. ground ginger

3 tsp. ground cloves

3 tsp. baking powder

1 tsp. salt

3 tsp. baking soda

3 tsp. vanilla

6–7 cups flour

1 can frosting of choice (or see Index for homemade frostings)

In a large bowl, cream together the sugar and oil. Add the remaining ingredients except the flour. Mix well. Gradually add the flour, blending well after each addition. Drop tablespoonfuls onto a nonstick cookie sheet, 2 inches apart. Bake at 350° for 8–10 minutes. Cool completely. Spread the frosting on one side of a pie and place another pie on top to form a sandwich cookie. Repeat for the remaining cookies.

Quick and Delicious Chocolate Whoopee Pies

2 chocolate cake mixes

⅔ cup vegetable oil

5 eggs

1 can frosting of choice (or see Index for homemade frostings)

Place the first four ingredients in a large mixing bowl and blend well. Drop by heaping tablespoonfuls, about 4 inches apart, onto a nonstick cookie sheet. Bake at 350° for 8–10 minutes. Cool. Spread the frosting on one side of a pie and place another pie on top to form a sandwich cookie. Repeat for the remaining cookies.

Red Velvet Whoopee Pies

1 cup butter (or margarine), melted

3 cups sugar

2 tsp. vanilla

4 eggs

2 cups milk

3 tbsp. red food coloring

5½ cups flour

½ cup unsweetened cocoa powder

3 tsp. baking soda

2 tbsp. apple cider vinegar

1 can frosting of choice (or see Index for homemade frostings)

Blend all the ingredients in a large mixing bowl. Drop by tablespoonfuls onto a nonstick cookie sheet. Bake at 350° for 10 minutes. Cool. Spread the frosting on one pie and place another pie on top to make a sandwich cookie. Repeat for the remaining cookies.

Zucchini Whoopee Pies

2 eggs

2 cups light brown sugar, packed

1 cup vegetable oil

1 tsp. baking soda

1 tsp. salt

1 tsp. baking powder

1 tsp. cinnamon

1 tsp. ground cloves (optional)

1 tsp. ground ginger (optional)

2 cups zucchini, peeled, cooked, and mashed

3½ cups flour

Fluffy Vanilla Frosting:

2 egg whites

2 tsp. vanilla

4 tbsp. flour

2 tbsp. milk

4 cups powdered sugar

1 cup shortening

In a medium mixing bowl, combine the eggs, brown sugar, oil, baking soda, salt, baking powder, and cinnamon, plus the cloves and ginger, if desired. Blend well. Mix in the zucchini and flour. Drop by teaspoonfuls onto a nonstick cookie sheet. Bake for 8–10 minutes. Cool. Meanwhile, combine the frosting ingredients and beat until smooth. Spread the frosting in between whoopee pies to make sandwich cookies.

Chewy Granola Bars

½ cup melted butter

½ cup light brown sugar, packed

1 cup light corn syrup

1 cup creamy peanut butter

2 tsp. vanilla

8 cups quick oats

⅔ cup chocolate chips (or raisins, nuts, or M&M's—optional)

Place the first five ingredients in a medium saucepan and melt over medium-low heat. Put the oatmeal in a large mixing bowl. Pour the warm mixture over the oatmeal and blend well. Spread on a greased 10" x 15" jelly roll pan. Bake at 350° for 15 minutes. Cool and cut into bars. Store in a tight container in a cool place.

Chocolate Chip Chews

½ cup margarine

¾ cup sugar

1 cup light brown sugar, packed

3 eggs, beaten

1 tsp. vanilla

½ tsp. baking soda

2½ cups flour

½ tsp. baking powder

1 tsp. salt

1 cup chocolate chips

1 cup nuts (optional)

In a large mixing bowl, cream together the margarine and the sugars. Add the remaining ingredients and mix well. Bake in a 9" x 13" baking pan at 350° for 25 minutes. Cool and cut into bars.

Couldn't Be Simpler Bars

½ cup butter, melted

1 cup graham cracker crumbs

1 cup sweetened coconut

1 cup butterscotch chips

1-14 oz. can sweetened condensed milk

1 cup chopped walnuts

1 cup semisweet chocolate chips

Pour the butter into 9" x 13" baking pan. Layer the next three ingredients evenly on top of the butter. Pour the milk over the entire mixture. Top with the walnuts and chips. Bake at 350° for 25 minutes or until golden brown and bubbly. Cool and cut into bars.

Crunch Bars

Bars:
- ½ cup butter
- ¾ cup sugar
- 2 eggs
- 1 tsp. vanilla
- ¾ cup flour
- ¼ tsp. baking powder
- ¼ tsp. salt
- ½ cup chopped walnuts (optional)
- 2½ cups mini marshmallows

Topping:
- 1½ cups chocolate chips (or ¾ cup chocolate chips and ¾ cup butterscotch chips)
- 1 cup creamy peanut butter
- 1½ cups Rice Krispies

In a mixing bowl, cream together the first four ingredients. Sift the flour, baking powder, and salt into the mixture. Stir in the walnuts, if desired. Spread the batter in a 9" x 13" baking pan. Bake at 350° for 15–20 minutes. Remove from oven and toss marshmallows over the top. Return to oven for 1 or 2 minutes, just until marshmallows melt. Cool for 30 minutes. Meanwhile, melt the chocolate chips and peanut butter in a saucepan and fold in the Rice Krispies. Spread on the topping, refrigerate for a half hour, and cut into squares.

Homemade Twix Bars

1 box Club Crackers
½ cup butter
1 cup graham cracker crumbs
¾ cup light brown sugar, packed
½ cup sugar
1 cup milk
1 egg
1 cup chocolate chips
¾ cup creamy peanut butter

Line a 9" x 13" baking pan with a single layer of crackers. In a saucepan, boil the butter, graham cracker crumbs, sugars, milk, and egg. Cook for 5 minutes. Pour over crackers. Add another layer of crackers. Melt chocolate chips and peanut butter in a saucepan and stir well. Spread over crackers and cool. Cut into bars.

Lemon Bars

Crust:
2 cups flour
1 cup margarine
½ cup powdered sugar

Filling:
4 eggs
2 cups sugar
6 tbsp. lemon juice
¼ cup flour
1 tsp. baking powder

Topping:
1 cup powdered sugar

In a small mixing bowl, blend the flour, margarine, and ½ cup powdered sugar. Press into a 9" x 13" baking pan. Bake at 350° for 20 minutes. Meanwhile, in a medium mixing bowl, blend the filling ingredients until smooth. Pour the filling over the baked crust. Return to oven and bake 25 minutes longer. Remove from oven and sift 1 cup of powdered sugar over the top. Cool and cut into bars.

Oatmeal Bars

1 cup butter
1 cup light brown sugar, packed
1 cup sugar
2 eggs
1 tsp. vanilla
1½ cups flour
1 tsp. baking soda
3 cups quick oats
¾ cup raisins
   (or chocolate chips)

Frosting:
   5 tbsp. butter
   1½ cups powdered sugar
   1 tsp. vanilla
   milk, if needed for
      consistency

In a large mixing bowl, blend all the batter ingredients. Spread the batter on a cookie sheet and bake at 350° for 20 minutes. Cool. Place the frosting ingredients in a medium bowl. Mix until the consistency becomes smooth and spreadable. Frost and cut into squares.

Oatmeal Date Bars

¾ cup butter
1 cup light brown sugar, packed
1 tsp. salt
½ cup honey
1 tsp. vanilla
½ cup nuts
1 cup chopped dates
1 cup sweetened coconut
4 cups quick oats

Melt the butter and brown sugar in a medium saucepan. Add the remaining ingredients in order and mix thoroughly. Pour into a 9" x 13" baking pan. Bake at 375° for 10–12 minutes or until a light golden brown. Cool slightly and cut into squares.

Cooking With the Fishers

Peanut Butter Bars

Batter:
½ cup butter, softened

½ cup sugar

½ cup light brown sugar, packed

½ cup creamy peanut butter

1 egg

1 tsp. vanilla

1 tsp. baking soda

¼ tsp. salt

1 cup chocolate chips

½ cup quick oats

1 cup flour

Icing:
½ cup powdered sugar

2 tbsp. creamy peanut butter

2 tbsp. (or more) milk

In a large mixing bowl, blend all the ingredients for bar mixture in the order shown. Spread in a greased 9" x 13" baking pan. Bake at 350° for 20–25 minutes or until light brown. Meanwhile, blend the icing ingredients in a medium mixing bowl. Cool the bars completely, ice, and cut.

Rhubarb Custard Bars

Batter:
2 cups sugar

7 tbsp. flour

1 cup sour cream

3 eggs, beaten

5 cups rhubarb, finely chopped

Crust:

2 cups flour

¼ cup sugar

1 cup butter

Topping:
6 oz. cream cheese

½ cup sugar

½ tsp. vanilla

1 cup Cool Whip

Stir all the batter ingredients together in a large mixing bowl, adding rhubarb last. Set aside. Combine the crust ingredients in a small mixing bowl and blend well to make a dough. Spread the dough into two 9" x 13" baking pans and pour the batter on top. Bake at 350° for 40–50 minutes. Remove from oven and cool. Meanwhile, mix the topping ingredients until well blended. Add the topping and cut into bars.

Rice Krispies Granola Bars

1¼ lb. marshmallows

¼ lb. (1 stick) butter, melted

¼ cup vegetable oil

½ cup honey

¼ cup creamy peanut butter

9½ cups Rice Krispies

5 cups quick oats

1 cup crushed graham crackers

1 cup chocolate chips

1 cup M&M's

Blend the marshmallows with the butter. Add the oil, honey, and peanut butter, and mix well. Set aside. In a very large mixing bowl, combine the Rice Krispies, oatmeal, crushed graham crackers, chocolate chips, and M&M's. Pour the marshmallow mixture into the Rice Krispies mixture and blend well. Spread onto two 9"x 13" cookie pans and cut into squares. Cool and serve.

S'mores Bars

3 cups graham cracker crumbs

¾ cup butter, melted

⅓ cup sugar

3 cups mini marshmallows

1 cup chocolate chips

In a large mixing bowl, blend the graham cracker crumbs, butter, and sugar. Press half of the mixture in a 9" x 13" baking pan. Sprinkle on the mini marshmallows and chocolate chips. Top with the remaining crumb mixture. Place plastic wrap over the mixture and press the ingredients firmly together. Remove plastic wrap and bake at 375° for 10 minutes. Press top firmly again. Cool. Cut into bars.

Sour Cream Raisin Bars

1 cup butter, softened
1 cup light brown sugar, packed
2 cups flour
2 cups quick oats
1 tsp. baking powder
1 tsp. baking soda
⅛ tsp. salt

Filling:
4 egg yolks
2 cups sour cream
1½ cups raisins
1 cup sugar
1 tbsp. cornstarch

Cream the butter and brown sugar in a large bowl. Beat in the flour, oats, baking powder, baking soda, and salt. Mixture will be crumbly. Set aside 2 cups of the crumb mixture. Press the remainder on a greased cookie sheet. Bake at 350° for 15 minutes. Cool completely. Meanwhile, place the filling ingredients in a medium saucepan and bring to a boil, stirring constantly. Pour the filling on top of the baked crumbs and sprinkle with the remaining crumbs. Bake for 15 minutes more. Cool and cut into bars.

CHAPTER 11

Breakfast Dishes

Granola

   14 cups quick oats
   1 cup light brown sugar, packed
   2 tbsp. dry milk powder
   1½ sticks butter, melted
   ¾ cup honey
   1 tsp. salt

Mix all the ingredients and bake in a 9" x 13" baking pan at 350° for ½ hour. Mixture will be crumbly. Store in an airtight container until ready to use.

Breakfast Casserole

12 slices of bread

2 lb. shaved ham

12 slices cheese (Colby, cheddar, Swiss, or other)

6 eggs

3 cups milk

1 tsp. dry mustard

1 tsp. onion powder

1 tsp. Season-All

1 tsp. oregano

Topping:

½ cup butter, softened

3 cups corn flakes

Place 6 slices of bread side by side in a 9" x 13" baking pan. Layer half of the ham over the top. Spread half the cheese slices on top of the ham. Repeat. In a mixing bowl, blend the eggs, milk, mustard, onion powder, Season-All, and oregano. Pour over all. Mix butter with corn flakes and add to pan. Bake at 350° for 45 minutes.

Breakfast Haystack

Sausage Gravy:
    1 lb. sausage meat

    water to cover

    2 tbsp. cornstarch

Haystack:
    1 lb. bacon

    4 medium potatoes, boiled and sliced

    ½ green bell pepper, diced

    1 small onion, diced

    dozen eggs

    6 toasted English muffins

Brown the sausage in a frying pan and drain off the grease. Add water to cover. Stir in the cornstarch and cook over medium heat until thickened. Keep the gravy warm until the eggs are done.

Fry the bacon until crisp. Drain off the grease and put aside. Break the bacon into small pieces and set aside. Pour 2 tbsp. of the bacon grease into the same frying pan and fry the potatoes, green peppers, and onions until softened. Lower heat and keep warm on the stove. In a large frying pan, scramble the eggs in 2 tbsp. of bacon grease. Add the bacon mixture. Serve on the muffins and top with sausage gravy. A prepared cheese sauce may be substituted for the sausage gravy.

Featherlight Pancakes

Pancake Mix:

8 cups flour

1 cup sugar

⅛ cup baking soda

2 tsp. salt

Pancakes:

2 eggs

¼ cup apple cider vinegar

2 cups milk

¼ cup vegetable oil

2¾ cups Pancake Mix (see above)

Blend the Pancake Mix ingredients. Place in a container with a tight lid and store in a cool dry place. To make pancakes, beat the eggs in a large bowl. Add the remaining ingredients and mix well. Lightly grease a frying pan or use a nonstick pan. Cook the pancakes until light golden brown on both sides. Serve with Pancake Syrup, page 114.

Whole Wheat Pancakes

Whole Wheat Pancake Mix:

12 cups flour (6 cups or less of this may be whole wheat flour)

¾ cup sugar

¾ cup baking powder

2 tbsp. salt

Pancakes:

1 cup milk

1 egg

1 cup Whole Wheat Pancake Mix (see above)

Blend the pancake mix ingredients. Place in a container with a tight lid and store in a cool dry place. For pancakes, combine the ingredients in a large bowl and stir well. Lightly grease a frying pan or use a nonstick pan. Cook the pancakes until golden brown on both sides. Serve with Pancake Syrup, page 114.

Syrupy Pancake Bake

Syrup:
  2 tsp. water
  1 cup light brown sugar, packed
  ½ cup butter

Top Layer:

1 egg	2 tbsp. butter, melted
1 scant cup milk	1 cup flour
½ tsp. salt	1 tbsp. baking powder
2 tbsp. sugar	

Bring the syrup ingredients to a boil in a small saucepan. Pour into a 9" x 13" glass pan. Set aside. In a large mixing bowl, combine all the top layer ingredients and beat well. Pour over the syrup. Bake at 350° for 30 minutes.

Golden French Toast

  ⅔ cup orange juice
  ⅓ cup milk
  1 tsp. grated orange peel (optional)
  4 eggs
  ¼ cup butter
  12 slices day-old French bread, sliced

Combine the orange juice, milk, orange peel, and eggs in a mixing bowl. Beat until well blended. Place the butter in a 9" x 13" baking pan and melt in the oven. Dip each slice of bread in the egg mixture and coat evenly. Place a single layer in the pan. Bake at 450° for 5–8 minutes. Remove from oven and turn slices over. Return to oven for 5–8 minutes longer. Serve with Pancake Syrup (see page 114).

Overnight Blueberry French Toast

12 thick slices of bread, cut in 1" cubes

1-8 oz. pkg. cream cheese, cut in ¾" cubes

1½ cups blueberries (fresh, frozen, or canned)

12 eggs

3 cups maple syrup

2 cups milk

Place half of the bread cubes in a buttered 9" x 13" baking pan. Distribute all of the cream cheese on top. Add the remaining bread cubes and the blueberries. Set aside. In a bowl, beat the eggs, syrup, and milk, and pour evenly in the pan. Cover and refrigerate overnight. Then cover with foil and bake at 325° for 30 minutes. Remove the foil and bake 20–30 minutes longer or until golden brown. Serve immediately.

Overnight Caramel French Toast

1 cup light brown sugar, packed	1 tsp. ground cinnamon
½ cup butter	
2 tbsp. light corn syrup	6 eggs
12 slices bread	1½ cups milk
¼ cup sugar	1 tsp. vanilla

Place brown sugar, butter, and corn syrup in a saucepan and bring to a boil over medium heat, stirring constantly. Remove from heat. Pour into a glass 9" x 13" baking pan. Top with 6 slices of bread. In a small bowl, combine the sugar and ½ tsp. of the cinnamon. Sprinkle half of this over the bread. Place the remaining 6 slices of bread on top. Sprinkle on the remaining sugar/cinnamon mix. Set aside. In a large bowl, beat the eggs, milk, and vanilla. Pour over the bread. Let soak for 8 hours, or overnight, in the refrigerator. Remove from the refrigerator 30 minutes before baking. Bake uncovered at 350° for 30–35 minutes. A great breakfast for overnight guests.

Pancake Syrup

1¼ cup light brown sugar, packed

¾ cup sugar

½ cup light corn syrup

1 cup cold water

1 tsp. vanilla (or maple flavoring)

Boil all the ingredients in a saucepan, stirring constantly. Reduce heat and simmer for 5 minutes on low. Remove from the heat and add the vanilla. Serve with pancakes or French toast.

CHAPTER 12

Canning & Preserving

Canning & Preserving

Ketchup

4 tbsp. dry mustard
¼ tsp. ground cloves
1 tsp. salt
½ tsp. cinnamon
1 pint apple cider vinegar
1½ quarts sugar
3 quarts tomato juice
½ Therm Flo (or Clear Jel)
¾ cup water

Cook the first seven ingredients over medium heat for 2 hours. Do not cover and do not allow it to boil. Stir the Therm Flo into the water and add to the ketchup to thicken. Pour the mixture into jars and seal.

Peach Jam

4 cups crushed peaches
2 tbsp. lemon juice
1 box Sure-Jell
7 cups sugar

Mix well and follow directions on Sure-Jell box. Jam can be canned or frozen.

Sweet Kosher Dill Pickles

approx. ½ bushel pickles (select long, thin pickles)

1 pkg. kosher dill pickle mix

18 cups water

6 cups sugar

4 cups white vinegar

2 tsp. salt

12 quart jars with lids

Wash and rinse canning jars. Set aside. Scrub the pickles with a vegetable scrubber and water to clean. Slice the pickles in rounds with the peel still on and put into jars. Combine the remaining ingredients and bring to a near boil. Pour liquid into the jars, stopping ¼ inch from the top.

To cold pack, put the jars in a 7- or 11-quart canner. Fill the canner with water, stopping ½ inch from the top. Bring the water to a boil and continue to boil for 10 minutes. Follow the lid directions on the pickle mix package.

Zucchini Relish

8 quarts zucchini, coarsely ground	2 tbsp. mustard seed
8 large onions, coarsely ground	5 cups sugar
1 cup salt	1 tsp. turmeric
3 cups apple cider vinegar	1 tbsp. celery seed
½ tsp. dry mustard	9 quart jars with lids

Combine zucchini and onions in a large bowl. Pour salt over the mixture and let stand for 20 minutes. Drain thoroughly and set aside. Combine the remaining ingredients in a large pot and bring to a boil. Add the drained zucchini mixture and boil for 7 minutes. Pour into hot sterilized jars and seal.

CHAPTER 13

Nonedible Household Formulas

Bubble Solution

⅓ cup liquid dish soap (or baby shampoo)
1¼ cups water
2 tsp. sugar
1 (or more) drops of food coloring (color of your choice)
pipe cleaners

Combine all the ingredients except the pipe cleaners, and pour into a nonbreakable bottle. To blow bubbles, use a pipe cleaner shaped into a circle at one end. Dip the circular end in the solution and blow bubbles.

Clay

1 cup cornstarch
1 cup salt
1 cup water, very warm

In a medium saucepan, combine all the ingredients and cook over medium heat until thickened. Remove from the stove and knead the mixture until it reaches the consistency of bread dough. Store in an airtight container.

Modeling Dough

1 cup flour
1 cup water
1 tbsp. vegetable oil
½ cup salt
1 tsp. cream of tartar
1-2 oz. bottle food coloring (color of your choice)

Place all the ingredients, except the food coloring, in a saucepan. Add the food coloring a little at a time until the desired color is achieved. Cook over medium heat until the mixture pulls away from the sides of the pan and has the consistency of dough. Remove from the pan and knead until cool. Can be kept in refrigerator for up to 3 months.

Amazing Cleaner

1 cup ammonia
½ cup apple cider vinegar
¼ cup baking soda
1 cup Stanley Degreaser
1-gallon bottle
water to fill

Combine all the ingredients, except water, in a 1-gallon container. Tighten the lid and shake well. Add water to 4 inches from the top. Shake well. Fill with water to make 1 gallon and shake well again. Use this all-purpose cleaner on countertops, kitchen cabinets, walls, and ceilings.

Nonedible Household Formulas

Bubble Bath

1 cup Dreft powder detergent
2 cups Epsom salts
quart container with lid

Pour the Dreft and Epsom salts into the container. Secure the lid and shake to mix.

Furniture Polish

1 quart water
2 tbsp. vegetable oil
2 tbsp. apple cider vinegar
1½-quart bottle

Pour the ingredients into the bottle and secure the lid. Shake well to mix.

Window Wash

1 pint rubbing alcohol
2 tbsp. ammonia
3 tsp. liquid detergent
3 drops food coloring (color of your choice)
1-gallon bottle
water to fill

Pour the first four ingredients into the bottle. Place the cap on the container and rock the bottle gently until well mixed. Add water to 4 inches from the top and shake slowly. Add more water to 2 inches from top. Shake again.

Recipe Index

Recipe Index

Recipe Index

Fisher
Produce Stand

Delicious fresh fruits and vegetables in season
• homemade soft pretzels and chips • fresh lemonade •

When you're in the Pennsylvania Dutch country, be sure to say hello!

John and Sylvia Fisher
Sarah Ann, Emma Mae, Amos,
David Paul, Mervin, and Aaron James

The Little Red Barn
3378 Old Philadelphia Pike
Ronks, PA 17572
(717) 768-7934
(We don't have a phone at home, but leave a message and we'll call you back.)

Or visit our shop at the Plain & Fancy Farm down the road
for homemade soft pretzels and hand-dipped ice cream.

www.plainandfancyfarm.com

Ask us for directions to the Home Farm for homemade root beer!

"Make sure to stop by when you're in the area. Bring your copy of *Cooking With the Fishers* along for an autograph! We love meeting new people!"

—The Fisher Family

GIVE THE GIFT OF

Cooking With the Fishers

Amish Family Recipes from
the Pennsylvania Farmland

TO YOUR FRIENDS AND COLLEAGUES

CHECK YOUR LEADING BOOKSTORE OR ORDER HERE

❑ **YES**, I want _____ copies of *Cooking With the Fishers* at $9.95 each, plus $4.00 shipping per book (Pennsylvania residents please add 60¢ sales tax per book). Canadian orders must be accompanied by a postal money order in U.S. funds. Allow 15 days for delivery.

My check or money order for $_____ is enclosed.

Please charge my: ❑ Visa   ❑ MasterCard
                           ❑ Discover   ❑ American Express

Name_____

Organization_____

Address_____

City/State/Zip_____

Phone_____ Email_____

Card #_____

Exp. Date_____ Signature_____

Please make your check payable and return to:
John Fisher
3378 Old Philadelphia Pike
Ronks, PA 17572

Call your credit card order to: 717-768-7934
www.sarah-maes.com